LISTEN
PRAYING IN A NOISY WORLD

LEADER GUIDE

RUEBEN P. JOB

LISTEN

PRAYING IN A NOISY WORLD

LEADER GUIDE
PAMELA HAWKINS, CONTRIBUTOR

Abingdon Press
Nashville

Listen
Praying in a Noisy World

Leader Guide
Pamela Hawkins, Contributor

This book is printed on acid-free, elemental chlorine-free paper.

Library of Congress Cataloging-in-Publication applied for.

ISBN 978-1-4267-8120-9

14 15 16 17 18 19 20 21 22 23—10 9 8 7 6 5 4 3 2 1
MANUFACTURED IN THE UNITED STATES OF AMERICA

CONTENTS

Preface 7

Introduction 9

Week 1: This Is My Son, Listen to Him 15

Week 2: Pray Like This. 25

Week 3: A Trusted Mentor 33

Week 4: Everyone Needs Help 43

Week 5: Flying Solo 51

Week 6: Getting into Position. 59

Prayers of Presence 69

Using *Listen: Praying in a Noisy World* as a
Congregational Resource. 77

Video Acknowledgments 79

PREFACE

*The skies were made by the L*ORD*'s word,*
       all their starry multitude by the breath of his mouth.
He gathered the ocean waters into a heap;
       he put the deep seas into storerooms.
*All the earth honors the L*ORD*;*
       all the earth's inhabitants stand in awe of him.
Because when he spoke, it happened!
       When he commanded, there it was!

Psalm 33:6-9

From the beginning of creation to the beginning of this day and any day, God communicates with us in myriad ways. Our task, for which we are equipped by the power and presence of the Holy Spirit, is to listen and respond to God.

In *Listen: Praying in a Noisy World,* Rueben P. Job gently assures us that learning to listen to God need not begin with guilt or frustration about how little we may be listening now, or even how little confidence we may have at being able to learn to listen. Rather, he makes a place for us beside him where learning to listen through prayer is safe, inviting, encouraging, and supported. He assures us that he is learning still because learning to listen to God through prayer is a life-long experience that begins and ends with God. Who better to both lead and join us in this journey of prayer and listening than Rueben P. Job, who has been spiritual guide and prayer companion for so many people around the world for more than six decades?

As for my own spiritual life and work, I can say without hesitation that Rueben has taught me to listen for and to God over and over again. Since our first meeting more than twenty years ago, I have had the privilege and gift of learning to pray in this noisy world because of his writing, preaching, praying, and guidance. And what Rueben has taught me about prayer, I have been able to share with others in the congregations, institutions, and communities in which I have served as pastor, author, teacher, and friend.

It is for this same purpose that this leader guide for the study *Listen: Praying in a Noisy World* is designed—to teach others to listen and pray. We are God's people, created to hear, trust, and follow God's ever-present, always-loving guidance. Prayer attunes us to God's will and Spirit despite competing noises in the world around us. Prayer clears a pathway toward God no matter the busy distractions and seductive detours that we encounter.

Prayer makes room in us to listen again to God—something we know how to do, deep within us, but often forget when caught up in the noise and detours of daily life. Both the individual and group experiences of *Listen: Praying in a Noisy World* are designed to help us remember and learn to listen to God once again. May all who choose to follow Rueben P. Job's spiritual guidance for transformation by the Spirit become listening and praying individuals, groups, and congregations who seek to follow Jesus.

Pamela Hawkins

INTRODUCTION

Listen: Praying in a Noisy World is a forty-day (six-week) prayer journey that guides both individuals and groups in learning how to listen, understand, and follow God's guidance and direction. Ideal for use during Lent or any time of year, the study invites participants to use the *Listen* prayer guide on their own throughout the week and then come together once a week to watch a video, discuss and share what they are learning, pray together, and have an opportunity to practice the featured prayer practice for that week. A group size of ten to twelve is recommended, but the material has been designed so that it may be adapted for larger groups as well.

As group leader, your role is to organize and facilitate the weekly group session using this leader guide and the companion DVD. This guide provides six session outlines for either a 60-minute or 90-minute group format:

60-Minute Format

Gathering and Welcome	5	minutes
Opening Worship	3	minutes
Video (viewing and discussion time)	18-20	minutes

Reflections on Weekly Reading	10	minutes
Prayer Practice in Community	15-17	minutes
Closing Worship	5	minutes

90-Minute Format

Gathering and Welcome	5	minutes
Opening Worship	3	minutes
Video (viewing and discussion time)	18-20	minutes
Reflections on Weekly Reading	10	minutes
Prayer Practice in Community	15-17	minutes
*Break	5	minutes
*Weekly Quotation Reflections	10	minutes
*Scripture Study	15	minutes
Closing Worship	5	minutes

As you can see, the 90-minute format is identical to the 60-minute format but contains three additional segments, which are marked with an asterisk. Feel free to adapt or modify either of these formats, as well as the individual segments and activities, in any way to meet the specific needs, learning styles, and preferences of your group. You also may wish to supplement with additional exercises or practices of your own choosing.

Here is a brief introduction to each segment of the session outline:

Preparation

The prayer pattern that group members will be using in their personal prayer time throughout the week, following the book *Listen: Praying in a Noisy World,* requires approximately fifteen to twenty minutes per day. This will serve as their preparation for the weekly group session. In addition to your own use of the daily prayer pattern, you will need some additional time each week for reading the group session outline in this guide, selecting activities, previewing the video segment (if desired), gathering any necessary items, and contacting group participants (optional but recommended). It is also suggested that you arrive about ten to fifteen minutes before the group session begins so that you can attend to room setup.

Gathering and Welcome (5 minutes)

Begin each week's session with time to pick up or make nametags so that group members can learn one another's names and greet one another. An introductory summary of the session is provided for you to read aloud or summarize. This material will help participants center on the purpose of the session as well as provide a time for settling in and reacquainting if participants do not know one another well.

Opening Worship (3 minutes)

After greeting participants, invite them into a time of worship. This will include praying in unison a communal version of the week's Prayer of Presence from *Listen: Praying in a Noisy World.* (You may copy and distribute the prayers found on pages 71-76 in this guide, or have the participants read the prayer each week from their books, replacing "I/me/my" with "we/us/our.")

You also will light a candle during this Opening Worship to remind participants of the presence of the Holy Spirit, following this with at least two minutes of silent prayer. Though it is recommended you lead this time of Opening Worship for the first session, you may want to invite participants to lead in later sessions.

Video (18-20 minutes)

Each week's session includes a video segment of approximately 10 minutes. View the video together and then use the questions provided for a time of discussion (for an additional 8-10 minutes).

Before beginning this discussion, inform participants that sharing is encouraged but not required. They always have permission to pass on speaking. Be prepared to share first to get the conversation going. Also, encourage participants to make room for everyone to share in the allotted time, and remind them to practice attentive listening when someone else is speaking. It will be important for you to manage each time of group discussion in order to stay on schedule.

Reflections on the Weekly Reading (10 minutes)

This activity invites participants to reflect more deeply on the Weekly Reading section from *Listen: Praying in a Noisy World*. Use the instructions and questions provided to shape this reflection time. Again, it may be helpful in the first two sessions to remind participants that sharing is optional and anyone may choose to pass during these group conversations. Remember, be prepared to share first if necessary.

Prayer Practice in Community (15-17 minutes)

This segment of the group session is one of the most important for supporting the readings in *Listen: Praying in a Noisy World*. Now that participants have spent the week learning and enacting the featured prayer method, Prayer Practice in Community extends and deepens individual prayer by offering time to use and discuss the prayer practice together.

You may want to reassure participants that there is no right or wrong way to pray, and that not everyone will be attracted to every form of prayer. Each week there may be participants who report that the prayer practice was enjoyable and helpful and others who say they did not enjoy it or find it comfortable. Encourage participants to be honest about their experiences, and be prepared to share examples of prayer that you may or may not prefer personally.

If you are using the 60-minute format, you will move directly to Closing Worship after completing Prayer Practice in Community. If you are using the 90-minute format, you will proceed with the following segments marked with an asterisk.

*Break (5 minutes)

Provide a short stretch break for participants. Let them know what time to be back in place for the rest of the session.

*Weekly Quotation Reflections (10 minutes)

During this segment, you will ask participants to review the quotations in this week's section of *Listen* and identify the quotation that most captured their attention. It may have stayed with them because of either a positive or negative response; either is fine to share. Participants who are willing to share will be invited to read the quotation and offer a brief explanation of why it caught their attention. It may be a word, phrase, sentence, or personal story or experience that was prompted by the quotation. While each person shares, others will be asked to listen and receive. For a session or two, be prepared to share first to provide a brief example. You also will need to manage the time so that all who wish to share can do so.

*Scripture Study (15 minutes)

For this segment, participants will locate a specified Daily Scripture reading, read it aloud two times, and then discuss it using the question provided or a prompt of your own. It will be helpful if you serve as a reader for at least the first group session. You may wish to let participants know in advance which reading will be highlighted each week.

Closing Worship (5 minutes)

Each group session closes with a segment of the Daily Prayer Pattern from *Listen* (adapted for a communal setting). First you will invite participants to a time of naming prayers of petition. Then you will say the Lord's Prayer in unison, and close by reading the blessing for the week.

* * *

As you prepare to lead your group in this journey of prayer, seeking God's presence and direction in your lives, remember that Jesus told us we would have all the help we need in discovering what we need to know in order to live fully as his disciples. He said, "The Companion, the Holy Spirit, whom the Father will send in my name, will teach you everything and will remind you of everything I told you" (John 14:26). We are not on our own in learning how to pray or how to discern God's will, and you are not alone in leading this group. Our Companion, the Holy Spirit, is our teacher and guide. It is God who chooses to make the way known to us, and it is God who does the revealing, leading, and instructing. The Master Teacher will guide you all along the way. What a wonderful promise as you begin your journey!

Week 1

THIS IS MY SON, LISTEN TO HIM

Preparation

In Advance

- Make a list of the names of all participants. In the days before the group gathers, spend time in prayer for each person. As you get to know group members, you will have specific prayers for each person; initially, simply hold them in prayer for whatever is taking place in their lives, and give God thanks for leading each one to be part of this group.
- E-mail or call each participant at least one week in advance of the first session to offer a personal welcome, to see if there are any questions about the meeting time or location, and to review what they are to read and do during the week prior to the first group session. (They should read the Introduction, How to Use This Book, and Week 1: This Is My Son, Listen to Him, pages 5-34.) Invite them to share any questions they may have about the prayer pattern they are to follow each day of the week. Remind participants to bring their books, a pen or pencil, and a journal or writing paper.
- Set aside time to review the session guide for Week 1, as well as read the Introduction, How to Use This Book, and Week 1 in *Listen.*

Plan to use the weekly prayer pattern and try the featured prayer practice in your own prayer time each day before the group meets.

- Make a copy of the Prayer of Presence for Week 1 for each group member so that you can pray it together in unison (see the back of this guide, page 71); or plan to have participants read the prayer from their books, replacing "I/me/my" with "we/us/our."
- Gather the materials needed:
  - ☑ Nametags and markers
  - ☑ Candle and lighter
  - ☑ Copies of the Prayer of Presence
  - ☑ Extra pens or pencils and writing paper
  - ☑ Extra copies of *Listen: Praying in a Noisy World* (optional)

On Site

- Arrive about 10-15 minutes before the group session begins so that you can be sure the room is set up as you would like. Be sure you have copies of the Prayer of Presence and the other materials needed for the session.
- On a chalkboard, whiteboard, or easel/flipchart, write the quotation from Rueben P. Job found on page 22 in *Listen: Praying in a Noisy World* (under "Prayer Practice") so that group members can easily see it as they enter.
- Prepare the materials needed for the session (see above).
- Once the room is ready and before the participants arrive, spend a few quiet moments in prayer for them and for the time that you will soon have together.

Gathering and Welcome (5 minutes)

Greet participants as they enter and ask them to make or pick up their nametags. Once all have arrived, remind them of why you have gathered. Read aloud or summarize:

This is a six-session group experience about learning how to listen and how to deepen our relationship with God through practices of prayer. These six sessions will serve as gathering points on our individual forty-day devotional journeys through which we will each be using Listen: Praying in a Noisy World *as our guide. Before each session we will complete a week of personal prayer practice using the book, and then we will meet here to reflect, discuss, and practice together what we have learned and experienced. At the center of these gatherings will be our shared desire to enhance our ability to hear and respond to God's guidance and to become more fully available to God.*

Because this is our first session together, let's spend a little time getting to know each other. (Invite group members to introduce themselves, briefly sharing about family, work, interests, and so forth.)

Each week we will begin with a simple time of worship, so let us enter into prayer.

Opening Worship (3 minutes)

Prayer of Presence (in unison)

> **Holy God**
> > **of unconditional love**
> > **and unlimited presence,**
> > **we come to make ourselves fully available**
> > **to you, your will, and your way.**
> **Speak to us gently and clearly,**
> > **for we are yours**
> > **and desire to hear, understand,**
> > **and be obedient**
> > **to your slightest whisper.**
> **Speak, for we are listening.**

Light of Life (light a candle)

Read aloud or summarize:

> *This candle represents the presence of the Holy Spirit, who is always with us and is ever prayerful for us. Let us live into*

the light that draws us away from the noisy world and toward a quiet space with God that we may learn to listen for the One who knows us as Beloved.

Silence in Community

Read aloud or summarize:

Now let us enter into silent prayer together, setting aside our mental calendars, schedules, and distractions as well as we can. Imagine handing over to God all that is weighing on your exterior life so that we can begin, together, to make room for the interior voice of God, who is waiting for this time with us.

Get as comfortable as you can and try to pay attention to your breath and heartbeat as we silently pray.

(Spend 1-2 minutes in communal silence.)

Amen.

Video (18-20 minutes total)

View the Video (10 minutes)

Discuss the Video (8-10 minutes)

Choose from the following questions to help group members reflect on the video. Be prepared to share first to help begin the discussion. Be sure to manage the time for the discussion so that you can move the session forward on time.

- Was there a comment or insight from today's video that really spoke to you?
- What were some of the reasons people gave for why they pray? Why do you pray?
- What is your earliest memory of prayer? Who taught you to pray?
- What can we learn from the variety of responses about where and when people pray? Where and when do you most like to pray?

Reflections on the Weekly Reading (10 minutes)

Invite participants to turn to the Weekly Reading on page 33 of *Listen: Praying in a Noisy World*. Invite everyone to listen carefully as you read the story aloud (or as a volunteer does so). Then guide a time of reflection about how the story relates to group members' lives. You may want to begin the reflection time with one of the following questions or one of your own. Be prepared to offer your response first as a model for sharing.

• What catches your attention in this story?
• In what ways does this story relate to the story of your life?

After each person who wishes to share has done so, ask group members to identify the main truth contained in this story. Discuss what is similar and different in what they have heard individually.

Prayer Practice in Community (15-17 minutes total)

This segment of the group session will focus on the week's prayer practice. The purpose of this section is to give group members time to talk about their individual experience of the practice, as well as to allow them to have a communal experience. Encourage group members to underline words or phrases in their books and to take notes in their books or personal journals during these discussions for future reflection. Be attentive to time management during this section so that all who wish to share have the opportunity to do so.

Time for Group Reflection (5 minutes)

Read aloud or summarize:

In each of our group sessions, we will reflect on and experience the prayer practice of the week. As you know, this week's practice is "Sitting in Silence." Let's begin by turning to page 22 in our books. We will review the instructions there and then discuss how you have experienced this prayer practice.

After everyone has had a minute to review the material on "Sitting in Silence," invite responses to the following questions:

- How did you experience "Sitting in Silence"? *(Encourage brief responses and model by sharing your own.)*
- What did you find to be difficult about this prayer practice? What did you find to be easy?
- How might this practice enrich your prayer life?
- What has helped you to grow in this practice?

Time for Group Practice (10-12 minutes total; 3-5 minutes of silence)

Read aloud or summarize:

Now we will spend time in prayer together, using the practice "Sitting in Silence." You may keep your books open to the instructions or close your eyes and listen as I read them. We will practice this prayer for 3-5 minutes.

Read aloud the following instructions slowly so that participants have time to respond to each part before you move to the next.

- *Begin by sitting quietly and comfortably.*
- *Allow the exterior voices to be silenced as you focus on the interior voice of God, who is seeking your attention.*
- *When your mind wanders, or as distractions catch your attention, gently return your focus to God's interior voice.*

Close the prayer time with "Amen." Then invite group members to briefly reflect on this communal experience using the following question or a prompt of your own. Be sure to watch your time.

- How did you experience this prayer practice today?

Note: If you are meeting for 60 minutes, move now to Closing Worship. If your session is 90 minutes, include the following elements marked with an asterisk before Closing Worship.

---

*Break (5 minutes)

*Weekly Quotation Reflections (10 minutes)

Ask group members to silently look back through Week 1 and identify the quotation that most catches and holds their attention. After giving a minute or two for this personal review, invite volunteers to read the quotation they have chosen and to say a few words about why. Again, be sure to model the desired response by sharing first. After all of those who desire to share have done so, bring this reflection time to a close.

*Scripture Study (15 minutes)

Ask group members to turn to the Daily Scripture for Friday of this week (Luke 9:28-35). After everyone has located the passage, ask one participant to read the text aloud while everyone listens closely. After this first reading is finished, allow a few moments of silence. Then ask another participant to read the same passage again.

Now lead a short discussion based upon this question or one of your own:

- What can this Scripture tell us about the importance of listening to God?

Be sure to properly manage the time for this discussion, and after 10-12 minutes draw the discussion to a close and prepare for Closing Worship.

Closing Worship (5 minutes)

Read aloud or summarize:

We will end our session by continuing our practice of prayer together. Let us first share any petitions we bring. As I lift up a category of petition, you are invited to name your prayers aloud or in silence. As we conclude our prayers of petition, we will join together in saying the Lord's Prayer (page 26 in your books), and then I will close with our blessing for the week.

Prayers of Petition

Offer at least a full minute of silence after you name each category of petition—or wait until it seems all have named the prayers of their hearts.

Let us pray.

For the world . . .
For the world's leaders . . .
For the world's people . . .
  For those whose lives touch ours today . . .
  For ourselves and those placed in our care . . .

The Lord's Prayer (in unison)

Our Father, which art in heaven,
Hallowed be thy Name.
Thy Kingdom come.
Thy will be done in earth,
As it is in heaven.

Give us this day our daily bread.
And forgive us our trespasses,
As we forgive them that trespass against us.
And lead us not into temptation,
But deliver us from evil.
For thine is the kingdom,
The power, and the glory,
For ever and ever.
Amen.

Blessing

Read aloud:

God of love and compassion, grant us grace to walk in companionship with you so that we may hear and respond to your call and may walk in faithfulness and peace this day and always.

Week 2

PRAY LIKE THIS

Preparation

In Advance

- In the days before the group gathers, spend time in prayer for each group member. Continue to give God thanks for leading each one to be part of this group, and lift up any concerns or joys they shared in the previous group session.
- E-mail or call participants to remind them of the week's assignment (Week 2: Pray Like This) and the time of the next group session. Also remind them to bring their books, a pen or pencil, and a journal or writing paper.
- Set aside time yourself to review the session guide for Week 2. Plan to use the daily prayer pattern and try the featured prayer practice in your own prayer time each day during the week before the group meets.
- Make a copy of the Prayer of Presence for Week 2 for each group member so that you can pray it together in unison (see the back of this leader guide, page 72); or plan to have participants read the prayer from their books, replacing "I/me/my" with "we/us/our."

- Gather the materials needed:
  - ☑ Nametags and markers
  - ☑ Candle and lighter
  - ☑ Copies of the Prayer of Presence
  - ☑ Extra pens or pencils and writing paper
  - ☑ Extra copies of *Listen: Praying in a Noisy World* (optional)

On Site

- Arrive about 10-15 minutes before the group session is to begin so that you can be sure the room is set up as you would like.
- Be sure you have copies of the Prayer of Presence and the other materials needed for the session.
- On a chalkboard, whiteboard, or easel/flipchart, write the quotation from Ben Campbell Johnson found on page 44 in *Listen: Praying in a Noisy World* (under "Daily Scriptures") so that group members can easily see it as they enter.
- Once the room is ready and before the participants arrive, spend a few quiet moments in prayer for them and for the time that you will soon have together.

Gathering and Welcome (5 minutes)

Greet participants as they enter and ask them to make or pick up their nametags. Once all have arrived, remind them of why you have gathered. Read aloud or summarize:

Welcome to the second week in our group experience of learning how to listen and how to deepen our relationship with God through practices of prayer. This week you have continued your individual forty-day devotional journeys using the guidebook Listen: Praying in a Noisy World. *Today we will pray, reflect, discuss, and practice together what we have learned and experienced during the week. With one another's help, we hope to enhance our ability to hear and respond to God's guidance and to become more fully available to God.*

Let us now enter into prayer together.

Opening Worship (3 minutes)

Prayer of Presence (in unison)

> **Loving God,**
> **Who understands before we form our prayers,**
> **Who hears when we call and translates our humble words**
>   **into beautiful hymns of gratitude and praise**
> **And responds to our uncertain cries for help**
>   **with assurance, peace, and palpable presence,**
>
> **Here we are, as fully in your presence**
>   **as we are able to be,**
> **Offering our fears, our needs, our hopes,**
>   **our love, and our lives,**
> **For we are yours and belong to no other.**

Light of Life (light a candle)

Read aloud or summarize:

> *This candle represents the presence of the Holy Spirit, who is always with us and is ever prayerful for us. Let us live into the light that draws us away from the noisy world and toward a quiet space with God that we may learn to listen for the One who knows us as Beloved.*

Silence in Community

Read aloud or summarize:

> *Now let us enter into silent prayer together, setting aside our mental calendars, schedules, and distractions as best we can. Imagine handing over to God all that is weighing on your exterior life so that we can begin, together, to make room for the interior voice of God, who is waiting for this time with us. Get as comfortable as you can and try to pay attention to your breath and heartbeat as we silently pray.*
> (Spend 1-2 minutes in communal silence.)
> *Amen.*

Video (18-20 minutes total)

View the Video (10 minutes)

Discuss the Video (8-10 minutes)

Choose from the following questions to help group members reflect on the video. As before, be prepared to share first to help begin the discussion. Be sure to manage the time for the discussion so that you can move the session forward on time.

- Was there a comment or insight from today's video that really spoke to you?
- How did those interviewed describe what prayer is? What is prayer to you?
- What were some of the different ways that people said they have learned to pray? What has helped you learn to pray?
- How did those interviewed express the importance of releasing our fears, needs, and hopes to God? What would you add to their observations?

Reflections on the Weekly Reading (10 minutes)

Invite participants to turn to the Weekly Reading on pages 51-52 of *Listen: Praying in a Noisy World.* Invite everyone to listen carefully as you read the story aloud (or as a volunteer does so). Then guide a time of reflection about how the story relates to group members' lives. You may want to begin the reflection time with one of the following questions or one of your own. Be prepared to offer your response first as a model for sharing.

- What catches your attention in this story?
- In what ways does this story relate to the story of your life?

After each person who wishes to share has done so, ask group members to identify the main truth contained in this story. Discuss what is similar and different in what they have heard individually.

Prayer Practice in Community (15-17 minutes total)

This segment of the group session will focus on the week's prayer practice. The purpose of this section is to give group members time to talk about their individual experience of the practice, as well as to allow them to have a communal experience. Encourage group members to underline words or phrases in their books and to take notes in their books or personal journals during these discussions for future reflection. Be attentive to time management during this section so that all who wish to share have the opportunity to do so.

Time for Group Reflection (5 minutes)

Read aloud or summarize:

This is the time of our session in which we will reflect on and experience the prayer practice of the week. As you know, this week's practice is "Releasing Our Fears, Needs, and Hopes." Let's begin by turning to page 36 in our books. We will review the description there and discuss how we have experienced this prayer practice.

After everyone has had a minute to review the material on "Releasing Our Fears, Needs, and Hopes," invite responses to the following questions:

- How did you experience "Releasing Our Fears, Needs, and Hopes"? *(Encourage brief responses and model by sharing your own.)*
- What did you find to be difficult about this prayer practice? What did you find to be easy?
- How might this practice enrich your prayer life?
- What could help you grow in this practice?

Time for Group Practice (10-12 minutes total; 3-5 minutes of releasing)

Read aloud or summarize:

Now we will spend time in prayer together, using the practice "Releasing Our Fears, Needs, and Hopes." You may keep your books open to page 36 or close your eyes and listen as I read the instructions. We will practice this prayer for 3-5 minutes.

Read aloud the following instructions slowly so that participants have time to respond to each part before you move to the next.

- *Begin by sitting quietly and comfortably.*
- *Invite the Holy Spirit to reassure you of God's constant and unfailing love and presence.*
- *In silence, name and place before God one or two fears or uncertainties in your life. Take these to God as soon as you are conscious of them.*
- *If you become anxious, return to the reassurance of God's love for you.*
- *In silence, name and place before God one or more needs that you have in your life. Again, entrust these to God.*
- *Finally, name and place before God some of your hopes. Be specific as you share these with God.*
- *Close by giving thanks for God's faithful presence, love, and care.*

Close the prayer time with "Amen." Then invite group members to briefly reflect on this communal experience using the following question or a prompt of your own. Be sure to watch your time.

- How did you experience this prayer practice today?

Note: If you are meeting for 60 minutes, move now to Closing Worship. If your session is 90 minutes, include the following elements marked with an asterisk before Closing Worship.

---

*Break (5 minutes)

*Weekly Quotation Reflections (10 minutes)

Ask group members to silently look back through Week 2 and identify the quotation that most catches and holds their attention. After giving a minute or two for this personal review, invite volunteers to read the quotation they have chosen and to say a few words about why. Again, be sure to model the desired response by sharing first. After all who wish to share have done so, bring this reflection time to a close.

*Scripture Study (15 minutes)

Ask group members to turn to the Daily Scripture for Monday of this week. After everyone has located the passage, ask one participant to read the text aloud while all listen closely. When this first reading is finished, allow a few moments for silent reflection; then ask another participant to read it again.

Lead a short discussion based upon this question or one of your own:

• What does this Scripture teach us about how to pray?

Be sure to manage the time for this discussion, and after 10-12 minutes, draw the discussion to a close and prepare for Closing Worship.

Closing Worship (5 minutes)

Read aloud or summarize:

We will end our session by continuing our practice of prayer together. Let us first share any petitions we bring. As I lift up a category of petition, you are invited to name your prayers aloud or in silence. As we conclude our prayers of petition, we will join together in saying the Lord's Prayer (found on page 26 in your books), and then I will close with our blessing for the week.

Prayers of Petition

Offer at least a full minute of silence following each category—or until it seems all have named the prayers of their hearts.

Let us pray.

For the world . . .
For the world's leaders . . .
For the world's people . . .
  For those whose lives touch ours today . . .
  For ourselves and those placed in our care . . .

The Lord's Prayer (in unison)

Our Father, which art in heaven,
Hallowed be thy Name.
Thy Kingdom come.
Thy will be done in earth,
As it is in heaven.

Give us this day our daily bread.
And forgive us our trespasses,
As we forgive them that trespass against us.
And lead us not into temptation,
But deliver us from evil.
For thine is the kingdom,
The power, and the glory,
For ever and ever.
Amen.

Blessing

Read aloud:
  We will accept and cherish our relationship as beloved and loving children of God as we live lives of prayer in God's presence today.

Week 3

A Trusted Mentor

Preparation

In Advance

- In the days before the group gathers, spend time in prayer for each group member. Continue to give God thanks for leading each one to be part of this group, and lift up to God any concerns or joys shared in the previous group sessions.
- E-mail or call participants to remind them of the week's assignment (Week 3: A Trusted Mentor) and the time of the next group session. Also remind them to bring their books, a pen or pencil, and a journal or writing paper.
- Set aside time yourself to review the session guide for Week 3. Plan to use the daily prayer pattern and try the featured prayer practice in your own prayer time each day during the week before the group meets.
- Make a copy of the Prayer of Presence for Week 3 for each group member so that you can pray it together in unison (see the back of this guide, page 73); or plan to have participants read the prayer from their books, replacing "I/me/my" with "we/us/our."

- Gather the materials needed:
  - ☑ Nametags and markers
  - ☑ Candle and lighter
  - ☑ Copies of the Prayer of Presence
  - ☑ Extra pens or pencils and writing paper
  - ☑ Extra copies of *Listen: Praying in a Noisy World* (optional)

On Site

- Arrive about 10-15 minutes before the group session is to begin so that you can be sure the room is set up as you would like.
- Be sure you have copies of the Prayer of Presence and the other materials needed for the session.
- On a chalkboard, whiteboard, or easel/flipchart, write the quotation from Rueben P. Job found at the top of page 65 so that group members can easily see it as they enter.
- Once the room is ready and before the participants arrive, spend a few quiet moments in prayer for them and for the time that you will soon have together.

Gathering and Welcome (5 minutes)

Greet participants as they enter and ask them to make or pick up their nametags. Once all have arrived, remind them of why you have gathered.

Read aloud or summarize:

This marks our half-way point through our six-week experience of learning how to listen and how to deepen our relationship with God through practices of prayer. You have completed your third week of your individual prayer journeys using the guidebook Listen: Praying in a Noisy World. *Today we will once again pray, reflect, discuss, and practice together what we have learned and experienced this week. It is my prayer that these group sessions are helping us to enhance our ability to hear and respond to God's guidance and to become more fully available to God.*

Let us join in prayer for our Opening Worship.

Opening Worship (3 minutes)

Prayer of Presence (in unison)

> *Lover of all who are lost,*
> *Uncertain and alone,*
> *Confused and frightened,*
> *Arrogant and disrespectful,*
> *Anxious and fearful,*
> *All who are seeking a safe and secure home,*
> *And all who are already*
> > *comfortably at home in your presence,*
>
> *Come to us now and*
> *Make yourself known to us*
> *As we seek to quiet the noise of the world,*
> *The anxiety of our hearts and minds,*
> *And the call of unfinished tasks*
> *So that we may recognize and welcome your voice,*
> *Embrace your presence,*
> *Understand your call,*
> *And invite you to change us more and more*
> *Into that wonderful image you have of us*
> *As your faithful, loving,*
> > *and obedient children.*

Light of Life (light a candle)

Read aloud or summarize:

> *This candle represents the presence of the Holy Spirit, who is always with us and is ever prayerful for us. Let us live into the light that draws us away from the noisy world and toward a quiet space with God that we may learn to listen for the One who knows us as Beloved.*

Silence in Community

Read aloud or summarize:

Now let us enter into silent prayer together, setting aside our mental calendars, schedules, and distractions as best we can. Imagine handing over to God all that is weighing on your exterior life so that we can begin, together, to make room for the interior voice of God, who is waiting for this time with us. Get as comfortable as you can and try to pay attention to your breath and heartbeat as we silently pray.

(Spend 1-2 minutes in communal silence.)

Amen.

Video (18-20 minutes total)

View the Video (10 minutes)

Discuss the Video (8-10 minutes)

Choose from the following questions to help group members reflect on the video. Be prepared to share first to help begin the discussion. Be sure to manage the time for the discussion so that you can move the session forward on time.

- Was there a comment or insight from today's video that really spoke to you?
- What are some of the ways the people interviewed said they listen for God? What helps you to listen for God?
- How has note-taking or journaling been a part of your own prayer practice?

Reflections on the Weekly Reading (10 minutes)

Invite participants to turn to the Weekly Reading on pages 67-68 of *Listen: Praying in a Noisy World*. Invite everyone to listen carefully as you read the story aloud (or as a volunteer does so). Then guide a time of reflection about how the story relates to group members' lives. You may want to begin the reflection time with one of the following questions or one of your own. Be prepared to offer your response first as a model for sharing.

- What catches your attention in this story?
- In what ways does this story relate to the story of your life?

After each person who wishes to share has done so, ask group members to identify the main truth contained in this story. Discuss what is similar and different in what they have heard individually.

Prayer Practice in Community (15-17 minutes total)

This segment of the group session will focus on the week's prayer practice. The purpose of this section is to give group members time to talk about their individual experience of the practice, as well as to allow them to have a communal experience. Encourage group members to underline words or phrases in their books and to take notes in their books or personal journals during these discussions for future reflection. Be attentive to time management during this section so that all who wish to share have the opportunity to do so.

Time for Group Reflection (5 minutes)

Read aloud or summarize:
In each of our group sessions, we reflect on and experience the prayer practice of the week. As you know, this week's practice is "Intentional Listening." Let's begin by turning to page 54 in our books. We will review the instructions there and then discuss how you have experienced this prayer practice.

After everyone has had a minute to review the material on "Intentional Listening," invite responses to the following questions:

- How did you experience "Intentional Listening"? *(Encourage brief responses and model by sharing your own.)*
- What did you find to be difficult about this prayer practice? What did you find to be easy?

- How might this practice enrich your prayer life?
- What could help you grow in this practice?

Time for Group Practice (10-12 minutes total; 3-5 minutes of listening and note-taking)

Read aloud or summarize:

Now we will spend time in prayer together using the prac-tice "Intentional Listening." You may keep your books open to the prayer practice on page 54 and take notes there during the prayer time or use the journaling pages at the end of the book. If you prefer, you may use separate paper instead. As I read the instructions for Intentional Listening, feel free to make any notes that come to mind as you listen and pray.

We will practice this prayer for 5 minutes.

Read aloud the following instructions slowly so that participants have time to respond to each part before you move to the next.

- *Begin by sitting quietly and comfortably with your paper and pen available.*
- *Invite the Holy Spirit to help you listen deeply for what God has for you to hear in the opening verses of Psalm 139. I will read the passage twice:*

> Lord, you have examined me. You know me.
> You know when I sit down and when I stand up.
> Even from far away, you comprehend my plans.

- *Now, in silence, listen not only for any obvious messages God is communicating to you through this Scripture but also for "subtle whispers." Make notes of anything that you hear or that comes to mind for you—any urgings, cautions, and encouragements.*
- *After you have recorded what you heard, make notes about any specific actions or responses you are prompted to take. Consider how you will respond to the signs, signals, and directions you are hearing. (Read the passage a second time.)*

Close the prayer time with "Amen." Then invite group members to briefly reflect on this communal experience using the following question or a prompt of your own. Be sure to watch your time.

- How did you experience this prayer practice today?

Note: If you are meeting for 60 minutes, move now to Closing Worship. If your session is 90 minutes, include the following elements marked with an asterisk before Closing Worship.

---

*Break (5 minutes)

*Weekly Quotation Reflections (10 minutes)

Ask group members to silently look back through Week 3 and identify the quotation that most catches and holds their attention. After giving a minute or two for this personal review, invite volunteers to read the quotation they have chosen and to say a few words about why. Again, be sure to model the desired response by sharing first. After all who desire to share have done so, bring this reflection time to a close.

*Scripture Study (15 minutes)

Choose the Daily Scripture for either Monday or Sunday of this week and ask group members to turn to it. After everyone has located the passage, ask one participant to read the text aloud while everyone listens closely. When this first reading is finished, allow a few moments of silence; then ask another participant to read the passage again.

Now lead a short discussion based upon this question or one of your own:

- What can this Scripture tell us about listening for God?

Be sure to manage the time for this discussion. After 10-12 minutes, draw the discussion to a close and prepare for Closing Worship.

Closing Worship (5 minutes)

Read aloud or summarize:

We will end our session by continuing our practice of prayer together. Let us first share any petitions we bring. As I lift up a category of petition, you are invited to name your prayers aloud or in silence. As we conclude our prayers of petition, we will join together in saying the Lord's Prayer (page 26 in your books), and then I will close with our blessing for the week.

Prayers of Petition

Offer at least a full minute of silence following each category—or wait until it seems all have named the prayers of their hearts.

Let us pray.

For the world . . .
For the world's leaders . . .
For the world's people . . .
 For those whose lives touch ours today . . .
 For ourselves and those placed in our care . . .

The Lord's Prayer (in unison)

> **Our Father, which art in heaven,**
> **Hallowed be thy Name.**
> **Thy Kingdom come.**
> **Thy will be done in earth,**
> **As it is in heaven.**
>
> **Give us this day our daily bread.**
> **And forgive us our trespasses,**
> **As we forgive them that trespass against us.**
> **And lead us not into temptation,**
> **But deliver us from evil.**
> **For thine is the kingdom,**

The power, and the glory,
For ever and ever.
Amen.

Blessing

Read aloud:

God of love beyond our comprehension, hold us close so that we may be as aware of the beat of your heart as we are of the beat of our own hearts as you guide us through the day.

Week 4

EVERYONE NEEDS HELP

Preparation

In Advance

- In the days before the group gathers, spend time in prayer for each group member. Continue to give God thanks for leading each one to be part of this group, and lift up any concerns or joys they shared in the previous group session.
- E-mail or call participants to remind them of the week's assignment (Week 4: Everyone Needs Help) and the time of the next group session. Also remind them to bring their books, a pen or pencil, and a journal or writing paper.
- Set aside time yourself to review the session guide for Week 4. Plan to use the daily prayer pattern and try the featured prayer practice in your own prayer time each day during the week before the group meets.
- Make a copy of the Prayer of Presence for Week 4 for each group member so that you can pray it together in unison (see the back of this guide, page 74); or plan to have participants read the prayer from their books, replacing "I/me/my" with "we/us/our."

- Gather the materials needed:
  - ☑ Nametags and markers
  - ☑ Candle and lighter
  - ☑ Copies of the Prayer of Presence
  - ☑ Extra pens or pencils and writing paper
  - ☑ Extra copies of *Listen: Praying in a Noisy World* (optional)

On Site

- Arrive about 10-15 minutes before the group session is to begin so that you can be sure the room is set up as you would like.
- Be sure you have copies of the Prayer of Presence and the other materials needed for the session.
- On a chalkboard, whiteboard, or easel/flipchart, write the quotation from Abraham Heschel found on page 70 ("Prayer is an invitation to God to intervene in our lives . . .") so that group members can easily see it as they enter.
- Once the room is ready and before the participants arrive, spend a few quiet moments in prayer for them and for the time that you will soon have together.

Gathering and Welcome (5 minutes)

Greet participants as they enter and ask them to make or pick up their nametags. Once all have arrived, remind them of why you have gathered.

Read aloud or summarize:

Our personal forty-day devotional journeys continue, and today we gather for the fourth week of our six-week group experience. We are learning so much about how to listen to and for God and how to deepen our relationship with God through different practices of prayer. This week's readings in our guide-book, Listen: Praying in a Noisy World, *have centered on the theme "Everyone Needs Help." Let us now enter into prayer together.*

Opening Worship (3 minutes)

Prayer of Presence (in unison)

> **God,**
> **Greater than anything we can imagine,**
> **Holiness purer and more brilliant than light,**
> **Mercy that forgives, redeems, and leads to righteousness,**
> **Love that accepts and embraces us just as we are,**
> **Grace that sustains and molds us into more than we are,**
> **Promised presence that will never forsake or leave us alone,**
>
> **We tremble in awe of such greatness and love,**
> **We fall on our knees in gratitude and humility;**
> **We yield our will to yours;**
> **We declare that we are yours alone**
> **and invite you to do with us what you will**
> **As we walk in the light and life**
> **of your unfailing presence.**

Light of Life (light a candle)

Read aloud or summarize:

> *This candle represents the presence of the Holy Spirit, who is always with us and is ever prayerful for us. Let us live into the light that draws us away from the noisy world and toward a quiet space with God that we may learn to listen for the One who knows us as Beloved.*

Silence in Community

Read aloud or summarize:

> *Now let us enter into silent prayer together, setting aside our mental calendars, schedules, and distractions as best we can. Imagine handing over to God all that is weighing on your exterior life so that we can begin, together, to make room for the interior voice of God, who is waiting for this time with us. Get as*

comfortable as you can, and try to pay attention to your breath and heartbeat as we silently pray.
  (Spend 1-2 minutes in communal silence.)
  Amen.

Video (18-20 minutes total)

View the Video (10 minutes)

Discuss the Video (8-10 minutes)

Choose from the following questions to help group members reflect on the video. As before, be prepared to share first to help begin the discussion. Be sure to manage the time for the discussion so that you can move the session forward on time.

- Was there a comment or insight from today's video that really spoke to you?
- What did those interviewed say about how prayer has helped them? How has prayer helped you?
- Those interviewed shared stories about praying and trusting God in difficult times. How has prayer helped you to trust God more?
- What are some of the different ways that those interviewed use meditation as a way to listen for God? How have you practiced or experienced meditation—both on Scripture and on God's presence in Creation? What have those experiences been like?

Reflections on the Weekly Reading (10 minutes)

Invite participants to turn to the Weekly Reading on pages 83-84 of *Listen: Praying in a Noisy World*. Invite everyone to listen carefully as you read the story aloud (or as a volunteer does so). Then guide a time of reflection about how the story relates to group members' lives. You may want to begin the reflection time with one of the following questions or one of your own. Be prepared to offer your response first as a model for sharing.

- What catches your attention in this story?
- In what ways does this story relate to the story of your life?

After each person who wishes to share has done so, ask group members to identify the main truth contained in this story. Discuss what is similar and different in what they have heard individually.

Prayer Practice in Community (15-17 minutes total)

This segment of the group session will focus on the week's prayer practice. The purpose of this section is to give group members time to talk about their individual experience of the practice, as well as to allow them to have a communal experience. Encourage group members to underline words or phrases in their books and to take notes in their books or personal journals during these discussions for future reflection. Be attentive to time management during this section so that all who wish to share have the opportunity to do so.

Time for Group Reflection (5 minutes)

Read aloud or summarize:

This is the time of our session in which we will reflect on and experience the prayer practice of the week. As you know, this week's practice is "Meditation." Let's begin by turning to page 70 in our books. We will review the instructions there and discuss how we have experienced this prayer practice.

After everyone has had a minute to review the material on "Meditation," invite responses to the following questions:

- How did you experience "Meditation"? *(Encourage brief responses and model by sharing your own.)*
- What did you find to be difficult about this prayer practice? What did you find to be easy?
- How might this practice enrich your prayer life?
- What could help you grow in this practice?

Time for Group Practice (10-12 minutes total; 5 minutes of meditating and note-taking)

Read aloud or summarize:

Now we will spend time in prayer together, using the practice "Meditation." We will use the Scripture reading for Saturday of this week, Philippians 2:1-5, found on page 80 in your books. Turn to this page, and feel free to make notes there during our time of prayer, or use the journaling pages or separate paper if you prefer.

We will practice this prayer for 5 minutes.

Read aloud the following instructions slowly so that participants have time to respond to each part before you move to the next.

- *Begin by sitting quietly and comfortably with your paper and pen available.*
- *Silently, read Philippians 2:1-5 several times. Make notes or underline anything that seems significant.*
- *Think deeply about the text. Write about your understanding of the passage.*
- *Pray about the passage's meaning and what it means for you specifically. Listen for God's voice.*
- *Sit silently, communing with God.*

Close the prayer time with "Amen." Then invite group members to briefly reflect on this communal experience using the following question or a prompt of your own. Be sure to watch your time.

- How did you experience this prayer practice today?

Note: If you are meeting for 60 minutes, move now to Closing Worship. If your session is 90 minutes, include the following elements marked with an asterisk before Closing Worship.

---

*Break (5 minutes)

*Weekly Quotation Reflections (10 minutes)

Ask group members to silently look back through Week 4 and identify the quotation that most catches and holds their attention. After giving a minute or two for this personal review, invite volunteers to read the quotation they have chosen and to say a few words about why. Again, be sure to model the desired response by sharing first. After all who desire to share have done so, bring this reflection time to a close.

*Scripture Study (15 minutes)

Choose the Daily Scripture for Wednesday or Thursday of this week and ask group members to turn to it. After everyone has located the passage, ask one participant to read the text aloud while everyone listens closely. When this first reading is finished, allow a few moments of silence; then ask another participant to read the passage again.

Now lead a short discussion based upon this question, or one of your own:

• What can this Scripture tell us about prayer and trusting God?

Be sure to manage the time for this discussion. After 10-12 minutes draw the discussion to a close and prepare for Closing Worship.

Closing Worship (5 minutes)

Read aloud or summarize:

We have arrived at the closing time of our session, and once again we will end in prayer together. Let us first share any petitions we bring. As I lift up a category of petition, you are invited to name your prayers aloud or in silence. As we conclude our prayers of petition, we will join together in saying the Lord's Prayer (found on page 26 in your books), and then I will close with our blessing for the week.

Prayers of Petition

Offer at least a full minute of silence following each category—or wait until it seems all have named the prayers of their hearts.

> *Let us pray.*
>
> *For the world . . .*
> *For the world's leaders . . .*
> *For the world's people . . .*
>> *For those whose lives touch ours today . . .*
>> *For ourselves and those placed in our care . . .*

The Lord's Prayer (in unison)

> **Our Father, which art in heaven,**
> **Hallowed be thy Name.**
> **Thy Kingdom come.**
> **Thy will be done in earth,**
> **As it is in heaven.**
>
> **Give us this day our daily bread.**
> **And forgive us our trespasses,**
> **As we forgive them that trespass against us.**
> **And lead us not into temptation,**
> **But deliver us from evil.**
> **For thine is the kingdom,**
> **The power, and the glory,**
> **For ever and ever.**
> **Amen.**

Blessing

Read aloud:
> *Creator of all that exists and lover of all you have made,*
> *Bless us with eyes to see your presence in the world you love,*
> *Ears to hear your tender voice of guidance,*
> *And courage to say, "Here we are, use us this day for we are yours."*

Week 5

FLYING SOLO

Preparation

In Advance

- As in previous weeks, spend time in prayer for each group member. Continue to give God thanks for leading each one to be part of this group, and lift up any concerns or joys they shared in the previous group session.
- E-mail or call participants to remind them of the week's assignment (Week 5: Flying Solo) and the time of the next group session. Also remind them to bring their books, a pen or pencil, and a journal or writing paper.
- Set aside time yourself to review the session guide for Week 5. Plan to use the daily prayer pattern and try the featured prayer practice in your own prayer time each day during the week before the group meets.
- Make a copy of the Prayer of Presence for Week 5 for each group member so that you can pray it together in unison (see the back of this guide, page 75); or plan to have participants read the prayer from their books, replacing "I/me/my" with "we/us/our."

- Gather the materials needed:
  - ☑ Nametags and markers
  - ☑ Candle and lighter
  - ☑ Copies of the Prayer of Presence
  - ☑ Extra pens or pencils and writing paper
  - ☑ Extra copies of *Listen: Praying in a Noisy World* (optional)

On Site

- Arrive about 10-15 minutes before the group session is to begin so that you can be sure the room is set up as you would like.
- Be sure you have copies of the Prayer of Presence and the other materials needed for the session.
- On a chalkboard, whiteboard, or easel/flipchart, write the quotation from Rueben P. Job found on page 97 in *Listen: Praying in a Noisy World* ("Be bold enough to ask God to transform your own life...") so that group members can easily see it as they enter.
- Once the room is ready and before the participants arrive, spend a few quiet moments in prayer for them and for the time that you will soon have together.

Gathering and Welcome (5 minutes)

Greet participants as they enter and ask them to make or pick up their nametags. Once all have arrived, remind them of why you have gathered.

Read aloud or summarize:

We are here for the fifth week of our six-week group experience guided by the book Listen: Praying in a Noisy World. *We have already spent time together reading, praying, and reflecting on a variety of themes related to listening and prayer. Today our theme is "Flying Solo" as we continue to learn how to deepen our relationship with God through prayer. Let us open with worship.*

Opening Worship (3 minutes)

Prayer of Presence (in unison)

> ***Creator God***
> ***Whose name is love,***
> ***Who made all that is***
> ***And is creating still,***
>
> ***Who nurtures and sustains all that is,***
> ***Seeks us with clear and tender invitation,***
> ***Desiring our constant attentiveness***
> >   ***so that we may hear every gentle word***
> >   ***of guidance, assurance, and love***
> ***As we are offered our full inheritance***
> >   ***as children of the living God,***
>
> ***Speak to us now as we listen***
> >   ***for your word of truth,***
> ***For we are yours and desire to***
> ***Live as your faithful children this day***
> >   ***and always.***

Light of Life (light a candle)

Read aloud or summarize:
>   *This candle represents the presence of the Holy Spirit, who is always with us and is ever prayerful for us. Let us live into the light that draws us away from the noisy world and toward a quiet space with God that we may learn to listen for the One who knows us as Beloved.*

Silence in Community

Read aloud or summarize:
>   *Now let us enter into silent prayer together, setting aside our mental calendars, schedules, and distractions as best we can.*

Imagine handing over to God all that is weighing on your exterior life so that we can begin, together, to make room for the interior voice of God, who is waiting for this time with us. Get as comfortable as you can, and try to pay attention to your breath and heartbeat as we silently pray.

(Spend 1-2 minutes in communal silence.)

Amen.

Video (18-20 minutes total)

View the Video (10 minutes)

Discuss the Video (8-10 minutes)

Choose from the following questions to help group members reflect on the video. As before, be prepared to share first to help begin the discussion. Be sure to manage the time for the discussion so that you can move the session forward on time.

- Was there a comment or insight from today's video that really spoke to you?
- What did those interviewed say about how God guides them? How has God guided you?
- What were some of the different ways that people talked about how prayer affects their work? How does prayer affect the work that you do?
- How did those interviewed express the importance of remembering God's love? Why is this an important part of prayer?

Reflections on the Weekly Reading (10 minutes)

Invite participants to turn to the Weekly Reading on pages 99-100 of *Listen: Praying in a Noisy World.* Invite everyone to listen carefully as you read the story aloud (or as a volunteer does so). Then guide a time of reflection about how the story relates to group members' lives. You may want to begin with one of the following questions or one of your own. Be prepared to offer your response first as a model for sharing.

- What catches your attention in this story?
- In what ways does this story relate to the story of your life?

After each person who wishes to share has done so, ask group members to identify the main truth contained in this story. Discuss what is similar and different in what they have heard individually.

Prayer Practice in Community (15-17 minutes total)

This segment of the group session will focus on the week's prayer practice. The purpose of this section is to give group members time to talk about their individual experience of the practice, as well as to allow them to have a communal experience. Encourage group members to underline words or phrases in their books and to take notes in their books or personal journals during these discussions for future reflection. Be attentive to time management during this section so that all who wish to share have the opportunity to do so.

Time for Group Reflection (5 minutes)

Read aloud or summarize:

Once more we come to the time to reflect on and experience the prayer practice of the week. As you know, this week's practice is "Remembering God's Love." Let's begin by turning to page 86 in our books. We will review the instructions there and discuss how we have experienced this prayer practice.

After everyone has had a minute to review the material on "Remembering God's Love," invite responses to the following questions:

- How did you experience "Remembering God's Love"? *(Encourage brief responses and model by sharing your own.)*
- What did you find to be difficult about this prayer practice? What did you find to be easy?
- What helps you remember God's unconditional love for you?
- What could help you grow in the practice of "remembering God's love"?

Time for Group Practice (10-12 minutes total; 5 minutes of remembering and note-taking)

Read aloud or summarize:

Now we will spend time in prayer together using the practice "Remembering God's Love." You may keep your book open to page 86, where this prayer practice is described, and take notes there, or you may wish to write your thoughts in a separate journal. We will practice this prayer for 5 minutes.

Read aloud the following instructions slowly so that participants have time to respond to each part before you move to the next.

- *Begin by sitting quietly and comfortably with your book or journal available.*
- *In your book or journal, write: "I am God's beloved child."*
- *In silence, repeat these words to yourself over and over for at least a minute, taking time to reflect on each word.*
- *Now, write a few sentences, a prayer, or a list of words that describe what God's love feels like to you. You may want to name people and places that remind you of God's love. Take your time with this. How do you describe God's love or what reminds you of God's love? Take about 2 minutes to do this.*
- *Now, close your eyes and imagine God saying to you: "You are my beloved daughter," or "You are my beloved son." Listen for these words of truth. Let them find a home in you.*

Close the prayer time with "Amen." Then invite group members to briefly reflect on this communal experience using the following question or a prompt of your own. Be sure to watch your time.

- How did you experience this prayer practice today?

> **Note: If you are meeting for 60 minutes, move now to Closing Worship. If your session is 90 minutes, include the following elements marked with an asterisk before Closing Worship.**

*Break (5 minutes)

*Weekly Quotation Reflections (10 minutes)

Ask group members to silently look back through Week 5 and identify the quotation that most catches and holds their attention. After giving a minute or two for this personal review, invite volunteers to read the quotation they have chosen and to say a few words about why. Again, be sure to model the desired response by sharing first. After all who wish to share have done so, bring this reflection time to a close.

*Scripture Study (15 minutes)

Choose the Daily Scripture for Tuesday, Thursday, or Saturday of this week and ask group members to turn to it. After everyone has located the passage, ask one participant to read the text aloud while all listen closely. When this first reading is finished, allow a few moments for silent reflection; then ask another participant to read it again.

Lead a short discussion based upon the following question or one of your own:

- What does this Scripture teach us about asking for and receiving guidance from God?

Be sure to manage the time for this discussion. After 10-12 minutes draw the discussion to a close and prepare for the Closing Worship.

Closing Worship (5 minutes)

Read aloud or summarize:

It is time for our Closing Worship and closing prayers. As in previous weeks, we will begin by lifting any petitions we bring. As I name a category of petition, you are invited to name your prayers aloud or in silence. As we conclude our prayers of petition, we will join together in saying the Lord's Prayer (found on page 26 in your books), and then I will close with our blessing for the week.

Prayers of Petition

Offer at least a full minute of silence following each category—or wait until it seems all have named the prayers of their hearts.

> *Let us pray.*
>
> *For the world . . .*
> *For the world's leaders . . .*
> *For the world's people . . .*
> > *For those whose lives touch ours today . . .*
> > *For ourselves and those placed in our care . . .*

The Lord's Prayer (in unison)

> **Our Father, which art in heaven,**
> **Hallowed be thy Name.**
> **Thy Kingdom come.**
> **Thy will be done in earth,**
> **As it is in heaven.**
>
> **Give us this day our daily bread.**
> **And forgive us our trespasses,**
> **As we forgive them that trespass against us.**
> **And lead us not into temptation,**
> **But deliver us from evil.**
> **For thine is the kingdom,**
> **The power, and the glory,**
> **For ever and ever.**
> **Amen.**

Blessing

Read aloud:

> *Faithful Guide and Companion, continue to speak to us the words of guidance, correction, encouragement, and love that we need. And send us to meet this day with your power and presence so that we may go where Jesus Christ leads us and to live as your faithful disciples all day long.*

Week 6

GETTING INTO POSITION

Preparation

In Advance

- Before your final group session, spend time in prayer for each group member. As you thank God for them, and for their commitment to this group experience, also pray that each person will draw closer to God in the days and weeks to come. Lift up any concerns or joys they shared in the previous group session.
- E-mail or call participants to remind them of the week's assignment (Week 6: Getting into Position) and the time of the next group session. Also remind them to bring their books, a pen or pencil, and a journal or writing paper.
- Set aside time to review the session guide for Week 6. Plan to use the daily prayer pattern and try the featured prayer practice in your own prayer time each day before the group meets.
- Make a copy of the Prayer of Presence for Week 6 for each group member so that you can pray it together in unison (see the back of this guide, page 76); or plan to have participants read the prayer from their books, replacing "I/me/my" with "we/us/our."

- Gather the materials needed:
  - ☑ Nametags and markers
  - ☑ Candle and lighter
  - ☑ Copies of the Prayer of Presence
  - ☑ Extra pens or pencils and writing paper
  - ☑ Extra copies of *Listen: Praying in a Noisy World* (optional)

On Site

- Arrive about 10-15 minutes before the group session is to begin so that you can be sure the room is set up as you would like.
- Be sure you have copies of the Prayer of Presence and the other materials needed for the session.
- On a chalkboard, whiteboard, or easel/flipchart, write the quotation from Rueben P. Job found on page 102 in *Listen: Praying in a Noisy World* ("How do we position ourselves today to receive God's love, presence, power, and grace?") so that group members can easily see it as they enter.
- Once the room is ready and before the participants arrive, spend a few quiet moments in prayer for them and for the time you will soon have together, asking for God to bless and keep each one after this last session is over.

Gathering and Welcome (5 minutes)

Greet participants as they enter and ask them to make or pick up their nametags. Once all have arrived, remind them of why you have gathered.

Read aloud or summarize:

This is our sixth and final session together as a group. Not only have we completed our forty-day individual prayer journeys, but today we also are concluding our communal journey in this study of prayer. Our group time may end today, but our individual practice of prayer will never end; and today's theme, "Getting into Position," reminds us of this truth and possibility. Let us open with worship.

Opening Worship (3 minutes)

Prayer of Presence (in unison)

> **God revealed in so many ways—**
> **The beauty and magnificence of creation,**
> **The words of prophet, priest, and servant,**
> **The life, death, resurrection of Jesus,**
> **The power and constant presence of your Spirit,**
> **The witness of your servant saints, and**
> **Your sustaining grace that gives us life—**
>
> **We bring ourselves into your presence**
> **Not to tell you what to do**
> **But to invite you to be our honored guest**
> **As we offer to you all that we are,**
> **All that we hope to become,**
> **And invite your transforming presence**
> **To shape us more and more into your**
> **Beloved and faithful children,**
> **For we are yours and we belong to you,**
> **Our faithful Savior and Guide.**

Light of Life (light a candle)

Read aloud or summarize:

> *This candle represents the presence of the Holy Spirit, who is always with us and is ever prayerful for us. Let us live into the light that draws us away from the noisy world and toward a quiet space with God that we may learn to listen for the One who knows us as Beloved.*

Silence in Community

Read aloud or summarize:

> *Now, for this last time together, let us enter into silent prayer, setting aside our mental calendars, schedules, and distractions*

as best we can. Imagine handing over to God all that is weighing on your exterior life so that we can begin, together, to make room for the interior voice of God, who is waiting for this time with us. Get as comfortable as you can, and try to pay attention to your breath and heartbeat as we silently pray.

(Spend 1-2 minutes in communal silence.)

Amen.

Video (18-20 minutes total)

View the Video (10 minutes)

Discuss the Video (8-10 minutes)

Choose from the following questions to help group members reflect on the video. As before, be prepared to share first to help begin the discussion. Be sure to manage the time for the discussion so that you can move the session forward on time.

- Was there a comment or insight from today's video that really spoke to you?
- What did those interviewed say about ways they hear from God or experience nudges from the Holy Spirit? What are some ways you hear from God?
- How did the video comments affirm the importance of attentiveness and expectancy? How can attentiveness and expectancy be a regular part of your daily prayer experience?

Reflections on the Weekly Reading (10 minutes)

Invite participants to turn to the Weekly Reading on pages 115-116 of *Listen: Praying in a Noisy World.* Invite everyone to listen carefully as you read the story aloud (or as a volunteer does so). Then guide a time of reflection about how the story relates to group members' lives. You may want to begin the reflection time with one of the following questions or one of your own. Be prepared to offer your response first as a model for sharing.

- What catches your attention in this story?
- In what ways does this story relate to the story of your life?

After each person who wishes to share has done so, ask group members to identify the main truth contained in this story. Discuss what is similar and different in what they have heard individually.

Prayer Practice in Community (15-17 minutes total)

This segment of the group session will focus on the week's prayer practice. The purpose of this section is to give group members time to talk about their individual experience of the practice, as well as to allow them to have a communal experience. Encourage group members to underline words or phrases in their books and to take notes in their books or personal journals during these discussions for future reflection. Be attentive to time management during this section so that all who wish to share have the opportunity to do so.

Time for Group Reflection (5 minutes)

Read aloud or summarize:

We now arrive at the time to reflect on and experience the prayer practice of the week. As you know, this week's practice is "Attentiveness and Expectancy." Let's begin by turning to page 102 in our books. We will review the description there and discuss how we have experienced this prayer practice.

After everyone has had a minute to review the material on "Attentiveness and Expectancy," invite responses to the following questions:

- How did you experience "Attentiveness and Expectancy"? *(Encourage brief responses and model by sharing your own.)*
- What did you find to be difficult about this prayer practice? What did you find to be easy?
- When has God captured your attention?
- What could help you grow in the practice of "attentiveness and expectancy" in prayer?

Time for Group Practice (10-12 minutes total; 5 minutes of prayerful attentiveness)

Read aloud or summarize:

Now we will spend time in prayer together using the practice "Attentiveness and Expectancy." You may wish to keep your book open to page 102 where this prayer practice is described.
We will practice this prayer for 5 minutes.

Read aloud the following instructions slowly so that participants have time to respond to each part before you move to the next.

- *Begin by sitting quietly and comfortably. Close your eyes if this will help you set aside distractions.*
- *Recall the past twenty-four hours and how you spent your time. Go slowly as you gently recreate the events and activities of this period of time.*
- *What event or activity most catches your attention as you remember the past day? A person, conversation, action, feeling? Choose one as you scan your memory.*
- *Spend time with this one experience, recalling as much as you can and revisiting the emotions and details. Pay attention to everything you can remember.*
- *Use your "spiritual eyes" to review this event. Be alert for why it stands out to you. Ask God to help you discover why this is, whether it is a positive or negative experience. Trust God with your attention.*
- *What connections do you see between this memory and your life right now? Reflect silently on these connections.*

Close the prayer time with "Amen." Then invite group members to briefly reflect on this communal experience using the following question or a prompt of your own. Be sure to watch your time.

- How did you experience this prayer practice today?

> Note: If you are meeting for 60 minutes, move now to Closing Worship. If your session is 90 minutes, include the following elements marked with an asterisk before Closing Worship.

*Break (5 minutes)

*Weekly Quotation Reflections (10 minutes)

Ask group members to silently look back through Week 6 and identify the quotation that most catches and holds their attention. After giving a minute or two for this personal review, invite volunteers to read the quotation they have chosen and to say a few words about why. Again, be sure to model the desired response by sharing first. After all who desire to share have done so, bring this reflection time to a close.

*Scripture Study (15 minutes)

Ask group members to turn to the Daily Scripture for Tuesday of this week. After everyone has located the passage, ask one participant to read the text aloud while everyone listens closely. When this first reading is finished, allow a few moments of silence; then ask another participant to read the passage again.

Now lead a short discussion based upon this question or one of your own:

- What can this Scripture tell us about the importance of being attentive and expectant in prayer so that we hear from God?

Be sure to manage the time for this discussion. After 10-12 minutes, draw the discussion to a close and prepare for Closing Worship.

Closing Worship (5 minutes)

Read aloud or summarize:

It is time for our final Closing Worship and prayers. We will begin, as we have each week, by lifting any petitions we bring.

As I name a category of petition, you are invited to name your prayers aloud or in silence. When we conclude our prayers of petition, we will join in the Lord's Prayer (page 26 in your books), and then I will close with the blessing for the week.

Prayers of Petition

Offer at least a full minute of silence following each category—or wait until it seems all have named the prayers of their hearts.

Let us pray.

For the world . . .
For the world's leaders . . .
For the world's people . . .
　For those whose lives touch ours today . . .
　For ourselves and those placed in our care . . .

The Lord's Prayer (in unison)

Our Father, which art in heaven,
Hallowed be thy Name.
Thy Kingdom come.
Thy will be done in earth,
As it is in heaven.

Give us this day our daily bread.
And forgive us our trespasses,
As we forgive them that trespass against us.
And lead us not into temptation,
But deliver us from evil.
For thine is the kingdom,
The power, and the glory,
For ever and ever.
Amen.

Blessing

Read aloud:

God of promise, power, and presence,
Be our ever-present Companion and Guide
So that this day and always
We may be your faithful servant children.

Prayers of Presence

Week 1

Holy God
of unconditional love
and unlimited presence,
we come to make ourselves fully available
to you, your will, and your way.
Speak to us gently and clearly,
for we are yours
and desire to hear, understand,
and be obedient
to your slightest whisper.
Speak, for we are listening.

Week 2

Loving God
Who understands before we form our prayers,
Who hears when we call and translates our humble words
*   into beautiful hymns of gratitude and praise*
And responds to our uncertain cries for help
with assurance, peace, and palpable presence,

Here we are, as fully in your presence
*   as we are able to be,*
Offering our fears, our needs, our hopes,
*   our love, and our lives,*
For we are yours and belong to no other.

Week 3

Lover of all who are lost,
Uncertain and alone,
Confused and frightened,
Arrogant and disrespectful,
Anxious and fearful,
All who are seeking a safe and secure home,
And all who are already
    comfortably at home in your presence,

Come to us now and
Make yourself known to us
As we seek to quiet the noise of the world,
The anxiety of our hearts and minds,
And the call of unfinished tasks
So that we may recognize and welcome your voice,
Embrace your presence,
Understand your call,
And invite you to change us more and more
Into that wonderful image you have of us
As your faithful, loving,
    and obedient children.

Week 4

God,
Greater than anything we can imagine,
Holiness purer and more brilliant than light,
Mercy that forgives, redeems, and leads to righteousness,
Love that accepts and embraces us just as we are,
Grace that sustains and molds us into more than we are,
Promised presence that will never forsake or leave us
alone,

We tremble in awe of such greatness and love,
We fall on our knees in gratitude and humility;
We yield our will to yours;
We declare that we are yours alone
and invite you to do with us what you will
As we walk in the light and life
of your unfailing presence.

Week 5

Creator God
Whose name is love,
Who made all that is
And is creating still,

Who nurtures and sustains all that is,
Seeks us with clear and tender invitation,
Desiring our constant attentiveness
 so that we may hear every gentle word
 of guidance, assurance, and love
As we are offered our full inheritance
 as children of the living God,

Speak to us now as we listen
 for your word of truth,
For we are yours and desire to
Live as your faithful children this day
 and always.

Week 6

God revealed in so many ways—
The beauty and magnificence of creation,
The words of prophet, priest, and servant,
The life, death, resurrection of Jesus,
The power and constant presence of your Spirit,
The witness of your servant saints, and
Your sustaining grace that gives us life—

We bring ourselves into your presence
Not to tell you what to do
But to invite you to be our honored guest
As we offer to you all that we are,
All that we hope to become,
And invite your transforming presence
To shape us more and more into your
Beloved and faithful children,
For we are yours and we belong to you,
Our faithful Savior and Guide.

Using
Listen: Praying in a Noisy World
as a Congregational Resource

As a congregational resource, *Listen: Praying in a Noisy World* offers a wide variety of options for use. First and foremost, because it is designed to be used at any time of year and in any liturgical season (for example, Lent), an entire congregation can be invited to share the forty days of reading and praying together as individuals and families. As they do so, some of the congregational uses can include one or more of the following, and for all of these, this leader guide will be helpful for facilitators:

- Have multiple small groups within the church use the study at the same time.
- Invite Sunday school classes, covenant groups, women's groups, and men's groups to use *Listen* and focus discussions on the material and prayer practices during the forty days.
- Include the featured prayer practice each week in the worship service.
- Create a preaching plan that focuses on the themes, Scriptures, and prayer practices for the six weeks of the study.
- Include excerpts and reflection questions from *Listen* in the church newspaper, bulletin, or website or other online congregational resources to help guide members of the community in their forty days of reading and prayer.
- Plan a one-night or one-morning congregational gathering or

workshop at the beginning of the forty days and another at the end of the forty days to reflect upon and share about the congregation's experience using *Listen*.

- Offer a weekly prayer group that focuses on the weekly prayer patterns or featured prayer practices in *Listen*.
- Create your own video segments for use in worship and/or at other times by interviewing members of the congregation on prayer.
- Invite church members of all ages to create "prayer visuals" for display throughout the church. Use creative prompts such as *What is prayer? What does prayer mean to you? What color or picture do you think of when you hear the word "prayer"?* Label each work of art with the individual's name and a title or description (include age for children). Host a prayer walk in which participants stop to pray as they view the artwork. Display the art throughout the forty-day experience of *Listen*.
- Create prayer stations in the sanctuary or elsewhere in the church with instructions and resources for different prayer methods and practices featured in the *Listen* resources—as well as others you might want to include. Invite church members to visit the prayer stations at set times, during prayer time in worship, or at other times.

Video
Acknowledgments

Shana Goodwin, Leticia Smith, and Dorris Walker are full-time employees of Thistle Farms, the social enterprise run by the women of Magdalene. Magdalene was founded in 1997 by Becca Stevens, an Episcopal priest, as a residential program for women who have survived prostitution, trafficking, addiction, and life on the streets. As employees of Thistle Farms, the women create natural bath and body products that are as good for the earth as they are for the body. Purchases of Thistle Farms products directly benefit the women by whom they were made. Magdalene stands as a witness to the truth that in the end, love is more powerful than all the forces that drive women to the streets.

Erron Kinney is a former American college and professional football player who was a tight end in the National Football League (NFL) for seven seasons during the early 2000s. Interested in fire safety since childhood, he became a firefighter in 2008 and was hired in 2013 as the first fire chief for the city of Mt. Juliet, Tennessee.

Gene Lovelace is a chaplain at Alive Hospice in Nashville, Tennessee, where he has served since 1996. Gene was one of this nonprofit agency's first full-time chaplains, and his work has included writing a standard of care titled "A Spiritual Guide at Alive Hospice: Caring Within a Community of Multi-Culture and Faith."

Kenny Martin is City Planner and Director of Economic and Community Development for the rapidly growing community of Mt. Juliet, Tennessee. Prior to accepting this position, he was Chief of Police for the city of Mt. Juliet and has served the city and citizens of Mt. Juliet for the last twenty-four years.

Neil Sharpe is a marriage and family therapist at Lantern Lane Farm in Mt. Juliet, Tennessee. Neil worked for twenty-seven years as an information technology business analyst before being called to leave the corporate world and help others find healing and restoration.

Cali VanCleave is a nine-year-old student who enjoys spending time with her friends and creating her own fashion designs. She is a new Christian who recently professed her faith through baptism.

Jenny Youngman is a singer/songwriter and writer in Nashville. When she's not performing or writing, she is managing the social lives of her four kids or serving the church her husband pastors.